No to Compulsory Veil
No to Compulsory Religion
No to Compulsory Government

Maryam Rajavi

No to Compulsory Veil,
No to Compulsory Religion,
No to Compulsory Government
Maryam Rajavi

A selection of six speeches by Maryam Rajavi from 2015 to 2017
in gatherings and conferences on the occasion of International
Women's Day.

ISBN: 978-2-9554295-5-6
(e-book)ISBN: 978-2-9554295-6-3

Published July 2017 by
National Council of Resistance of Iran
15, rue des Gords 95430 Auvers sur Oise- France

Table of Contents

Struggle Against the Religious Tyranny Ruling Iran: A Mission for All Women

Speech by Maryam Rajavi in a roundtable discussion with members of parliament, scholars and women's rights activists
Tirana – March 2017

In a roundtable discussion on March 2017, on the occasion of the International Women's Day, entitled, «Women in Leadership, the Experience of the Iranian Resistance», Maryam Rajavi shared the experience of the women of the Iranian Resistance with participants.
Following are her remarks:

The Iranian women's struggle for freedom and equality has lasted one-and-a-half centuries, as confirmed by the Iranian and Western historians who have studied the developments of the past 150 years in Iran. Over this span of time, we have seen women leaders who rose up and proved their competence in various arenas, despite the reigning culture and policies of tyranny and misogyny. This phenomenon was most significantly demonstrated in women's courageous participation in the anti-dictatorial struggles over this period.

Women's struggle is essentially the best and most comprehensive indicator of progress in a given society. How can we measure the advances of a society towards real progress and development? The answer is to the extent it endeavours to achieve freedom and equality.

In the absence of gender equality, any political, economic or social progress is ineffective, fleeting, or reversible.

From this vantage point, the uprisings which led to the 1979 overthrow of the Shah in Iran marked a major leap forward because of women's remarkable and extensive participation in street demonstrations. This new phenomenon unveiled the Iranian people's widespread desire for progress. At the same time, it revealed a shocking contradiction: On the one hand, the ruling regime quickly adopted regressive and despotic policies and brought about appalling backwardness. On the other hand, Iranian society as a whole was seeking freedom and democracy, and sought social progress and advancements. Such contradiction led in the first step to a major clash. The barbarity and savagery of the new regime drenched the Iranian revolution in blood.

The role of women in the Iranian Resistance

Women's active participation in the confrontation with the mullahs' religious fascism formed the cornerstone and foundation of resistance against the regime. Quantitatively, women's participation in this struggle had been extensive since the outset. Qualitatively, they were brave, efficient and selfless. Tens of thousands of women have been tortured or executed in the struggle against the ruling fundamentalist regime, in particular in the 1980s. If women were not powerfully motivated, and if they had not set their sights on a bright and magnificent horizon, they would have definitely been intimidated by the merciless tortures and massacres, unprecedented in our contemporary history. Instead, the clampdown made them even more determined and resolute.

Women's role rapidly became more pronounced in the developments of post-revolution Iran. They became the pivotal force of the movement. Today, women hold key leadership positions in the resistance movement. They make up more than 50 percent of the members of the Resistance's parliament-in-exile.

The guiding principles of women's role in the Iranian Resistance can be summarized as follows:

Firstly, the struggle of the women of this movement for equality has been deeply intertwined with the broader struggle for freedom in Iran. Therefore, it has targeted the ruling dictatorship - a religious tyranny, while combating its compulsory religious edicts, misogyny and inhumane discrimination.

Secondly, women have waged a foundational struggle against objectification, while defying the gender-based ideology that forms the central tenet of inequality.

Thirdly, women have recognized their mission and mandate in leading this movement, and in doing so have discovered that a hegemonic women's role provides a liberating force, propelling women forward, and have subsequently implemented that role in practice.

Fourthly, these revolutionary women have linked their struggle to that of the resistant, equality-seeking men of the movement. They view support for those men in the struggle against inequality and against patriarchal thinking and culture as a key responsibility.

The emergence of Islamic fundamentalism

Iranian women have gained many valuable experiences in their struggle against the ruling religious tyranny, which is the source of Islamic fundamentalism. A cursory review of the origins of fundamentalism and its essence will aid us in explaining this point more clearly.

Beginning in the late 18th century and early 19th century, as major political, social and technological developments in the world cast their shadow over the geographical region that hosts most of the Islamic countries – extending from North Africa to the Caucuses, Central Asia and the Indian Ocean, the peoples of those regions rose up to change their destiny. They sought freedom, independence, rule of the law, as well as economic and social progress.

Why did this wave wash over Islamic countries? Why was a limited, but strongly resonating part of this wave driven towards extremism? How did «Asian despotism» emerge in the cloak of Islamic fundamentalism to confront this ubiquitous wave of social awakening? Several series of factors apparently worked hand in hand to create the wave of social awakening in Muslim countries, while at the same time driving a major share of it towards extremism:

-Major industrial, technological leaps along with the increasing globalization of trade, production and money markets created a strange and unexpected image of a new world, shocking the nations of this region and launching an awakening process and eager propensity to find access to the gifts of the developed Western world.

-The populations of these countries grew dramatically, as did their commercial relations with the West, specifically with capitalism, shaking the foundations of the old traditions, relations and institutions.

-At the same time, Islam's deep and longstanding influence on the culture, ideology, traditions, institutions and laws ruling the relations of the people in this region naturally affected every development in these countries.

Against this backdrop, several destructive factors laid the groundwork for the emergence of Islamic fundamentalism. Ignorance, lack of education and backwardness are, of course, some of the contributing factors. Additionally, however, are the interference and mistakes committed by western governments in these countries, whose catastrophic effects, including invasions, displacement of populations, and destruction of national social institutions, produced profound antipathy and resentment toward the West, as acknowledged today by many western analysts and even politicians. Western governments supported dictatorial regimes, in the process destroying the middle class, producing uneven economic and social growth, and eliminating nationalist parties and freedom-loving movements.

The world of Islam also witnessed major events of the 20th century, each of which prepared the grounds for the emergence or enhancement of Islamic fundamentalism, including the formation of Pakistan and then Bangladesh, the Middle East war, the Soviet invasion of Afghanistan, and the collapse of the Soviet Union.

The defining impact of the Iranian regime

None of them, however, so impacted the expansion and empowerment of fundamentalism as did the rise to power of the medieval mullahs in Iran. Khomeini and his allies' appropriation of power in exceptional and unique historical circumstances, marked the exact moment when Islamic fundamentalism as we know it entered the global stage. This was a horrendous, power-hungry and profoundly misogynous force founded on religious discrimination. It institutionalized its backward sharia laws as a mechanism to establish a religious tyranny, and became a model of governance for fundamentalist groups.

In reality, dictatorships like the previous regime of Iran were too weak and corrupt to stand against the waves of people demanding freedom, particularly against the powerful forces of women and youths. Instead, religious fundamentalists set about cracking down on and suppressing them.

The essence of fundamentalism

At its core, what does Islamic fundamentalism seek to confront? Is it the Islamic world lining up against the West, or specifically against Christianity and Judaism? The answer is NO. Is it, as the fundamentalists claim, enmity to the manifestations of the

modern world? No, otherwise, they would not have used to such an extent the internet, cell phones and bank transactions, or resorted to nuclear technology and advanced weaponries.

In truth, the real dispute is not between Islam and Christianity, Islam and the West, or Shiites and Sunnis. It is, rather, a confrontation between freedom and subjugation, and between equality and injustice. Islamic fundamentalism, in essence, represents a backlash against the overwhelming tendency of the peoples of the region, especially women and youth, towards freedom, democracy and equality.

In 1965, when establishing the People's Mojahedin Organization of Iran (PMOI), its founder, Mohammad Hanifnejad, said the line was drawn not between theists and atheists, but between the oppressed and the oppressors. In fact, the PMOI has challenged Islamic fundamentalism and religious deception since its inception. Three years before Khomeini seized power in Iran, the Iranian Resistance's Leader Massoud Rajavi, at the time imprisoned by the previous dictatorship, reiterated that religious fundamentalism was the real threat to the Iranian people's freedom-loving movement.

11

And it was this threat that rapidly emerged in all Muslim communities.

Enmity against women

It should be clear why fundamentalism focuses its wrath and violence against women, because women's emancipation was the central theme of the vast tide of people seeking a new order, freedom and equality. Women emerged as a new force in the 1979 revolution in Iran and played a remarkable role. That role rapidly evolved and became more prominent after the revolution, becoming the pivotal force of the struggle. They were in the frontlines of resistance in torture chambers, of the demonstrations during the 2009 up rising, and they were in the front lines of the command structure in the National Liberation Army of Iran.

In contrast to this, enmity to women lies at the heart of Islamic fundamentalism and suppression of women is the central component of the suppression of the entire society.

Why did the mullahs need to revive the laws of past millennia in the final years of the 20th Century? Why did they commit such inconceivable crimes under the name of Islam?

Because they faced a widespread, common desire that could only be confronted and contained by naked oppression. The Iranian regime resurrected or invented most of the cruelties and evil crimes that were later copied and borrowed by fundamentalist groups and individuals. Such atrocities even found their way into the laws of a few Islamic countries. The Iranian Resistance with women as its vanguard launched its fight against a regime which was the enemy not only of the people of Iran, but also the main threat to the entire Middle

East.

We have been warning for three decades that Islamic fundamentalism is a global threat. Over the past 15 years, this threat has emerged in the form of terrorism and conflicts in the Middle East. Today, we see that European capitals have not remained immune from terrorist crimes carried out by fundamentalists. Wherever fundamentalists guided by the mullahs enter the scene, their terrorism and destruction quickly begins. In conclusion, I would like to underscore that it is imperative for the entire world to confront this ominous phenomenon. The mullahs of Iran and their fundamentalist disciples are the enemy not only of the people of Iran, but also the enemies of all Middle East nations and the entire world. In particular, fundamentalism targets and jeopardizes all the achievements that women have made to date. Therefore, confronting the Iranian regime should be the immediate goal of the women's struggle the world over. Women's international sisterhood and solidarity demands that we all support the fight against the fundamentalist regime of Iran.

Women's Leadership and a Generation of Men Committed to Freedom and Equality

Speech by Maryam Rajavi, International Women's Day Tirana – March 2017

On the eve of the International Women's Day, a grand meeting entitled "Women in Political Leadership" was held on March, 2017, in Tirana, Albania.

The ceremony featured Maryam Rajavi as the keynote speaker as well as a number of distinguished politicians, personalities and women's rights activists from different countries who addressed the conference and declared solidarity with the Iranian Resistance and its pioneering women.

The presence of a group of 1000 Iranian Resistance's women who resisted 14 years in camps Ashraf and Liberty in this IWD ceremony was the focal point of attention and speeches in this conference.

In addition to speeches, the IWD celebration also featured musical performances and documentary video clips on the plight of Iranian women and their 150-year struggle for freedom.
Following are Maryam Rajavi's remarks:

I am delighted that this year, we are observing International Women's Day in the presence of a group of the 1,000 pioneering women of Ashraf, whose defense against the attacks of the clerical regime in previous years comprised part of our sisters' struggle worldwide.

The PMOI's safe and secure relocation from Camp Liberty and out of Iraq, which was accomplished collectively as an organization, was a heavy blow to the mullahs' regime. As demonstrated in their fierce missile attacks, they wanted to destroy the pivotal force of the alternative to their regime. But they failed.

That said, I would like to extend my earnest appreciation to the government and people of Albania for their great initiative. Albania serves as an example of freedom and humanitarianism in today's world.

I must also pay sincere tribute to the honorable and inspiring women from around the world, a number of whom are present here today, who lent their invaluable support and assistance to the women of Ashraf.

Solidarity in recent years with the one thousand women of Ashraf has been one of the most brilliant and effective women's projects and one of the world's most glorious solidarity movements.

I hail all these dear sisters who participated in this solidarity campaign. I would like to use this opportunity to thank the Iranian supporters of Ashraf who played a key role in this endeavour. I expect that they will continue and expand their efforts in support of the Iranian women's struggle for freedom and equality.

The significant role of Iranian women

The people of the world know the Iranian regime for its export of terrorism, war and fundamentalism and for its efforts to make nuclear weapons. As a result, two major realities have gone less noticed:

First is the fact that the Iranian regime, in conjunction with its export of terrorism and fundamentalism to the region, is also the prime advocate of misogyny in those countries. Therefore, it should be considered as the most dangerous threat to women's achievements in today's world.

Second is the fact that defiant women have had a significant role in the fight against Iran's ruling fundamentalists. The fact that women bear the brunt of repression in Iran, reveals that repression as the regime's defensive tactic against the existential threat it feels from women.

The imposition of the mandatory veil and flagrant discrimination in educational and vocational arenas are simply efforts to enchain women; otherwise the mullahs would not be able to preserve their power. They will be toppled by these women and by the general Iranian populace.

From another angle, women have proven themselves in their effective and growing role in the struggle against the mullahs' religious tyranny: for example, in the confrontations with the Revolutionary Guards, in their unprecedented resistance in the regime's torture chambers and dungeons, through their presence in the frontlines of anti-regime demonstrations, in organizing teachers, workers' and other protests; in organizing and leading an international social and political movement against the religious fascism ruling Iran, as well as by taking on key responsibilities in the organized movement of the Iranian Resistance.

The point I would like to make is that for decades, women's struggles and International Women's Day have focused on the elimination of inequality and violence against women as their objective. Today, however, women have a mission beyond these goals, of saving humanity from fundamentalism and terrorism.

The experience of the Iranian Resistance

Please allow me to explain in this regard the experience specific to the Iranian Resistance. In the 1990s, we faced the issue of women's leadership on various levels, which changed the organizational structure of our movement. Our women had stepped onto a path without precedent or examples from the past. So, they decided to remove anything that bore any sign of inequality, anything that ignored women or obstructed their collective participation, and built new relations in their stead.

They overcame the monster of internalized disbelief as their main obstacle, and began to cultivate a sense of self-confidence and to believe their own abilities. They liberated themselves from the clutches of the mindset that viewed them as a mere commodity. Instead of passivity and evading responsibility, they chose to assume their responsibilities. They shunned fear of failure and weakness in the face of difficulties and created new relations based on camaraderie and sisterhood.

The first decade of the new millennium, which saw the US invasion of Iraq in 2003 followed by the Iranian regime's interventions, witnessed a difficult situation for our movement. The regime, with the assistance of its puppet government in Iraq, laid siege to Camp Ashraf and initiated a ruthless campaign to destroy the PMOI. At the same time, the mullahs took advantage of Western governments' policy of appeasement and launched a full-fledged offensive aimed at annihilating the movement. Women's leadership faced yet another challenge in such excruciating circumstances.

The question is: how did they overcome the customs and traditions deeply entrenched through thousands of years, and how did they manage to carry on and move forward?

Actually, this transformation, since its inception in our movement, did not aim to simply switch the leadership roles of women and men. Women's participation at various leadership and management levels is indeed a step forward, but it is not sufficient to create a new culture unless it is accompanied by a fundamental revolution permeating the entire culture and relations between men and women. And so long as it does not establish equality and solidarity, its achievements would tend to be reversible.

A new message

And this is exactly where the novel message of our Resistance lies: women's leadership can become a lasting institution and tradition only when it is supported by men who have faith in, and are committed to, the ideal of equality, and who accept their rightful responsibilities in this regard. Without the men who cherish and rise up to realize the cause of equality, women's leadership cannot become reality. The experience of women's leadership in our movement became possible with the role that men played as pioneers in this new world. Therefore, I address you, my dear brothers, and say:

The path you have paved over the past three decades is a cause of pride and honor, not only for myself and all of us, but for our nation and for a humanity that thirsts for freedom and equality. These liberated men formed new collective relations among themselves. They eagerly and passionately defended the cause of women's equality everywhere and endorsed their leadership. They created new values and ethics based on honesty, self-sacrifice, and giving priority to others. They firmly rejected the outlook that sees women as mere commodities. Such relations led to the fostering of far greater solidarity among men themselves.

Equal participation of women and emancipation of men

Therefore, women's equal participation in leadership is not a process that could be realized without men's emancipation. How can half of any community break the chains of subjugation and compulsion, while the other half remains in darkness?

The experience of our movement proved that women's leadership grants them the status of equal, responsible human beings. This, coupled with men's acceptance of women's leadership, creates a liberating mechanism that leads to equality and better relations. As a result, sisterhood, brotherly relations, and solidarity evolve to new heights.

This means that relations of both women and men become free from negative judgment and competition, as well as narrow-

mindedness and prejudice. Everyone sees other individual's advances not as an obstacle but as a new opportunity for his or her own progress. Yes, in such an emancipated and free world, the advances of men and women do not contradict each other, but are essential complements.

In fact, the men of this movement have a message of emancipation for Iranian society as a whole. The message is a call to our sons, brothers and fathers in Iran to rise up in defense of freedom and equality if they want to realize the Iranian people's freedom. Their emancipating message is «brotherhood,» a message that has gotten lost in today's world. In this way, women's leadership in the Iranian Resistance movement is the name and manifestation of a revolution that has created new relations based on genuine equality. I must stress that such equality is not confined to legal and political equality, or to equal opportunities. Rather, it requires the enhancement of human solidarity whereby women take ownership of their own fates, and men who believe in the cause of equality develop a productive, creative and active character in themselves.

Such new or novel relations, free of so many fetters and restrictions, produced enormous energy within a besieged movement, enabling it to uphold its celebrated steadfastness. As a result: You, the PMOI, were able to sustain the bastion of freedom and equality for many years in the face of nine attacks and bloodbaths and two hostage-takings, during 677 days of sonic, psychological torture and despite eight years of an inhuman siege.

At the international level, too, you defeated, one after the other, the blacklisting --at the mullahs' behest -- of the PMOI in Europe and the U.S. You proved the legitimacy of this Resistance in over 20 courts.

Therefore, the important conclusion about the developments of these years is that the steadfastness of the bastions of freedom in Ashraf and Liberty was made possible by such women and men, as were the Resistance's advancements in all political, legal and international arenas. This is the illuminating experience of the amazing abilities present in the leadership of women and in relationships based on equality. This novel phenomenon is represented in 1,000 pioneering women and a generation of men who seek freedom and equality.

Here I'd like to congratulate Massoud Rajavi for training and educating such a generation of women and men, who have spawned this enormous transformation in the history of the Iranian resistance movement and movements of peoples around the region.

So, it is right to say that the 21st century belongs to women. We must remember, however, that women's leadership is genuine when it leads the way towards humane relationships and genuine equality between men and women, and towards engagement with a long line of men who believe in equality.

A regime based on inequality marginalizes women. A regime that prevents the participation of a great portion of the populace in running their country's affairs, ends up with absolute tyranny, totalitarianism, monopoly of power, secret decision-making, corruption and repression, with the country's wealth and resources wasted.

Women's leadership is the solution to this dilemma, which has become universal in today's world. I must stress that where democracy does not exist, it cannot be achieved without women's equal participation in leadership.

The courageous undertaking of an adventure

In 2011, the late Madam Danielle Mitterrand sent a message to the women and men of Ashraf: «My dear friends in Ashraf, the future is made by the sacrifices you make, but this is not enough. Everyone must always remember the message of hope to humanity written in your blood and the example you have set for the oppressed.» [1]

Françoise Héritier, the prominent French anthropologist, also referred to the experience of women in Ashraf and Liberty, saying: «If this experience proves to be successful, it would set a model for humanity. This will be a message to women. An unnatural reaction has been imposed on every woman since childhood, for her to say that she is never going to be able to do things because everything she does is under the dominance of men. Now, this new message tells women not to surrender to such impositions, but that they must accept to courageously undertake an adventure.» [2]

Yes, it is about undertaking the adventure with courage. And this is what the women of Ashraf have done.

1. Read the complete text of Danielle Mitterrand›s message in the Appendices.

2. Read the complete text of message by Françoise Héritier in the Appendices.

Hail to the proud women of Ashraf who sacrificed their lives during this glorious steadfastness. Hail to Saba Haft Baradaran, Asieh Rakhshani, Nastaran Azimi,and Mahdieh Madadzadeh, to Zohreh Qa'emi and Giti Givechian, to Kolsum Sarahati, Pouran Najafi and Nayyereh Rabii, among many others. Those who hoisted a flag carried before them by a long list of heroines and pioneers like Asharf Rajavi, Fatemeh Amini, Marzieh Oskouii, Azam Rouhi Ahangaran, Nosrat Ramezani, Azadeh Tabib, Tahereh Tolou, Mahin Rezaii, Nasrin Parsian, Batoul Rajaii, Farideh Vanaii and the countless brave women who were slain on the path of the Iranian people's freedom and emancipation.

Women pioneer change

For the free Iran of tomorrow, we place great emphasis on women's equality with men and believe it is imperative for the overthrow of the religious dictatorship and is the guarantee for democracy; equality in the eyes of the law and judiciary, equality in the family, equality in economic opportunities, and active and equal participation in political leadership.

We espouse women's freedom and freedom of choice, including her freedom to choose her attire and her career, and she must also enjoy the right to divorce.The ruling regime in Iran is the cause of retardation and decadence of Iranian society and all the countries in the region.

It is the main cause of coercion in religion, the source of sectarianism among Shiites and Sunnis, and the advocate of stoning and inhumane laws under the pretext of implementation of the laws of Islam.

Ask the nations of the Middle East, who is the main enemy of

their life and subsistence?

Ask the people of Syria, which regime provides the primary assistance to Bashar Assad in killing half a million of their compatriots, many of whom are also rendered homeless?

Ask Syrian women, which evil force has taken away the homes of millions of Syrian women? Which regime created a bloodbath in Aleppo through its Revolutionary Guards and foreign militias and killed so many innocent children in cold blood?

We see the mullahs' agents and emissaries even in the Balkans, spreading fundamentalist ideas that pave the way for terrorism. All of these catastrophes and calamities are spread by the religious dictatorship ruling Iran. The women of Iran are burning today by the millions in the fire of repression, a plethora of crushing restrictions, poverty and deprivation. They and the displaced women of Syria and Iraq face a common enemy. Therefore, they have a common struggle and a common goal: the overthrow of the Iranian regime.

Change in Iran – and today I say, change throughout the world-- is realized by women blazing the trail.

And finally, I would like to address you, the freedom-loving women and men of Iran.

Freedom can be achieved by making sacrifices and paying the necessary price. It can be achieved by courageous rebellions against repression and humiliation. It can be achieved by resisting with bravery and hope, and by a relentless struggle to establish one thousand Ashrafs, and one thousand bastions of rebellion and struggle.

Yes, we can and we must overthrow the velayat-e faqih religious dictatorship, and we can and we must achieve freedom for Iran and establish a free republic based on equality.

This is the test and responsibility of each and every one of us.

To achieve this and to create a new order, we must rise up.

The Velayat-e Faqih Regime, Enemy of Women

Speech on International Women's Day, «Women United Against Fundamentalism» conference
Paris, Maison de la Mutualité – February 27, 2016

A grand gathering was held on the eve of the International women's day on Saturday, February 27, 2016, in Paris. Entitled, «Pledge for Parity: Women United Against Fundamentalism,» the conference featured Maryam Rajavi and a number of political dignitaries, intellectuals, prominent personalities and activists of the equality movement from 26 countries in four continents.

Amongst the speakers were Linda Chavez, former White House Director of Public Liaison and US expert to UN Sub-Commission on Human Rights; Rama Yade, former

French Minister of Human Rights; Ingrid Betancourt, former Colombian presidential candidate; Rita Süssmuth, former President of German Bundestag; Ranjana Kumari, Director of the Centre for Social Research and 5th winner of the Lotus Leadership Award from India; Nagham Ghaderi, Vice-President of Syrian National Coalition; Rashida Manjoo and Yakin Ertuk, former UN Special Rapporteurs on Violence against Women; Christine Ockrent, French journalist, writer and renowned TV commentator; Beatriz Becerra, member of the European parliament from Spain; Stefania Pezzopane, Italian Senator; Margarita Duran Vadell, Spanish Senator; Fatiha Bakkali on behalf of women legislators from Morocco; Najima Thay Thay, former Minister of Education and Youth from Morraco; Anissa Boumediene, former first lady of Algeria, Islamic scholar and jurist; Azza Heikal, Egyptian writer and professor of Arab Academic University affiliated with the Arab League and a leader of women's council of Arab tribes; Majedeh Novaishi, Vice-President of Arab Women Representatives Coalition from Egypt; Drita Avdyli, former Deputy Minister and current Chairwoman of National Chamber of Mediation, Diana Culi, writer journalist and politician, Sevim Arbana, founder of organization Useful to Albanian Women from Albania; a delegation of jurists, including Fatoumata Dembélé Diarra (Mali), Kristy Brimelow QC and Sara Chandler (Britain), Chair of Human Rights Commission of Federation of European Bar Associations; Maria Candida Almeida, Attorney General Deputy in the Supreme Court (Portugal); Zinat Mir-Hashemi, member of the National Council of Resistance of Iran, member of the Central Committee of the Cherik-hay-e Fedaii Organization

(OPFGI); Safora Sadidi, member of PMOI Central Council; and a number of chairs of associations and communities and youth supportive of the Iranian Resistance.
Following are Maryam Rajavi's remarks:

March 8th calls for a salute to the women who strive for equality and freedom. We pay tribute to women who have risen up for a glorious tomorrow and a better world that will not know the meaning of submission, despair and helplessness.

Today, the courageous women of Iran who are languishing in prisons and the brave mothers who have been relentlessly staging protests in front of Evin Prison celebrate this day with us.

We also salute the women who pioneered the struggle against two dictatorships in Iran. And hail to the oppressed women of Syria who are steadfast despite their great pain and suffering under bombardments, or in ISIS criminal attacks, or in foreign lands without shelter. So far, more than 400,000 Syrians, including countless women and children, have been killed.

Indeed, why must so much suffering continue? And why does the world acquiesce to the crimes of the mullahs' regime in Syria? For those who strive for the cause of gender equality, what duty is more urgent than solidarity with the millions of women whose lives are ablaze in Syria?

For our sisters all over the world, what struggle is more important than confronting the source of war and bloodshed in the Middle East, namely the Velayat-e Faqih regime ruling Iran?

Therefore, I call on every one of you and all activists of the equality movement the world over to come to the aid of the suffering women of Syria, Iraq and Yemen.

Misogyny in the mullahs' Sharia

Fundamentalism is a proliferating cancer threatening everyone. Extremism under the banner of Islam – including Daesh - has spread all over the world; the primary victims are women. It is, therefore, necessary to recognize the epicenter of this great calamity, how to uproot it, and to determine the role of women in this endeavor. For this reason, I would like to elaborate on an issue today about which there is little awareness: the suppression of women in Iran and the Iranian women's resistance against the regime.

A fundamentalist regime has been ruling Iran for more than three decades. Its most basic characteristic is enmity to women. In the past three, four decades, nowhere in the world have women been tortured and executed in such great numbers or assaulted in prisons as they have in Iran.

Let us first address this situation in the regime's laws and the basic elements of its Sharia.

Article 167 of the Iranian regime's Constitution stipulates: «The judge must try to base the verdict of each dispute on the codified laws. If his attempt fails, he should issue the verdict on the case by referring to reputable Islamic sources or religious rulings (fatwas).»

The article grants judges freedom of action to cite religious rulings in issuing their verdicts. These fatwas, however, are only those contained in Tahrir-ol Vasileh, a book on Khomeini's decrees. A considerable portion of this book is devoted to the means and methods of male domination, imposing inequality on women, sanctioning polygamy and even legitimizing anti-human treatment of women and girl children.

The book contains a number of fatwas on taking female slaves and justifies slavery of women in the mullahs' Sharia. In other words, Khomeini defended slavery in the 20th century. In dozens of other decrees, Khomeini has permitted men to have any number of temporary wives. Again in the 20th century, he has allowed the mullahs' followers to take women as war booty and own them as property.

Khomeini emphasized in his book that «some human rights cannot be proven unless by a man's testimony, and the testimonies of two women cannot replace one man's testimony.»

In another instance, he wrote, «The testimony of a woman is not acceptable by itself. Even the testimonies of one man and six women cannot be accepted... Even the testimonies of eight women are not acceptable.»

Still further, Khomeini has justified sexual abuse of girls under nine years of age and even infants. The book also contains a number of rulings on marrying minor girls. In several edicts, Khomeini has degraded the value of a woman's marriage to a financial deal, thus insulting women's worth and dignity.

The common practice of rape and violence against women is a product of such Sharia. The UN Special Rapporteur on Violence against Women, Ms. Yakin Ertürk, provided a clear picture of this in her 2005 report on Iran.

Widespread addiction of women and their misery is yet another product of the mullahs' corrupt Sharia. This is why we say Velayat-e Faqih is the enemy of women.

Meanwhile, Khomeini and his mullahs have been injecting this ideology into the minds of fundamentalist groups in other countries over the past three decades. They have funded and organized many of these groups. Over the years, and particularly over the past two years, this phenomenon has been permeating and spreading in countries across the Middle East and Africa and emerging in various forms, ranging from Daesh, the Taliban, and Boko Haram to the Iranian regime's militias in Iraq, Yemen and Lebanon.

Look at Daesh's treatment of women today, which is justified by invoking Islamic edicts. Look at how they take the Yazidi women and girls as slaves. These are exactly the same as the rulings written in Khomeini's book from which I cited a few examples.

Whether Sunni or Shiite, these groups share several basic elements:

-Imposing their religion by force;

-Carrying out the mullahs' Sharia laws;

-Ignoring borders and committing genocide and terrorist assassinations;

-Enmity toward the West;

-Using excommunication to eliminate opponents;

-Misogyny; and

-Establishing a tyrannical state under the name of a Caliphate, Islamic State or Velayat-e Faqih. In his book entitled «The Islamic State,» Khomeini formally defined his desired regime as a caliphate.

In fact, Iran's ruling mullahs, Daesh and like-minded groups have disguised this absolutely vicious and misogynous savagery as Islam, while anything that promotes compulsion and force and denies popular suffrage and free choice, is not Islam; it is anti-Islam. And anything that denies women's equal rights has no place in Islam.

We will not tolerate violation of women's rights under the guise of religion or under any other pretext. We advocate democratic Islam in the face of extremism, fundamentalism and exploitation of religion. With the emancipating word of «equality» and with women's active and equal participation in political leadership, we seek in the name of women, to turn this century into the century of women's emancipation and of humankind's liberation.

Rule of violence against women

Velayat-e Faqih is the enemy of women because it rules by constant violence and suppression against women. In addition to 74 forms of torture practiced in the regime's political prisons, a large number of young women were raped before execution according to a shameful fatwa. Rape of young men and women occurred on an extensive scale during 2009.

The regime has executed thousands of women for their political activities. Here, at this very moment, I am thinking of

Fatemeh Mesbah, only 13 at the time of her execution. I am thinking of Mojgan Jamshidi, only 14 when she was executed, and Noushin Imami who was only 16. I remember women who died under torture and women who were pregnant when sent before the firing squads.

Not one, not 100, not 1,000, but thousands of women were executed, sent to the gallows or tortured to death, stopping thousands of beating hearts yearning for freedom and equality. The victims were thousands of determined human beings, each of whom was a world of compassion and knowledge.

In recent years, a large number of women have been executed on trumped up charges or for petty crimes. At least 64 women have been hanged in Iran under Rouhani[1]. Reyhaneh Jabbari[2], that courageous young woman, and so many other Reyhanehs whose names are unknown. These unheard voices, however, must not be underestimated. The tears that no one saw and the moaning that was suffocated must not be underestimated. These are the echoes of a raging storm that will ultimately eradicate women's enemies.

Compulsory veil

Another area of violence and compulsion in Iran is the

---

1. According to data collected by the Women›s Committee of the National Council of Resistance of Iran, at least 64 women were executed in Iran from September 9, 2013 until the end of December 2015. The NCRI Women›s Committee estimates that the actual number of women executed must be much higher because «most executions in Iran are carried out secretly without anyone knowing except those who carry it out.-http://www.women.ncr-iran. org/documents/2158-63-women-executed-in-iran-under-rouhani

2. Reyhaneh Jabbari, born on November 6, 1987, was executed on October 15, 2014. The young woman was 19 when she was assaulted by Morteza Abdul-Ali Sarbandi, an Intelligence Ministry official. While defending herself, she stabbed the assailant which led to his death. Reyhaneh was detained in prison for seven years and ultimately hanged. The execution, carried out on an unfair verdict issued only to provide immunity for agents of the Intelligence Ministry, outraged the general public.

mandatory dress code or Hijab. Since the early days of Khomeini's rule, Iranian women protested against compulsory veiling. At the time, the PMOI women actively participated in demonstrations against compulsory veiling.

In his memoirs, Rouhani has admitted how, as Khomeini's representative in the Army's politico-ideological bureau, he initiated enforcement of the veil in the offices of the Armed Forces, and described how he personally went to all the offices to make the veil mandatory for all women[3].

A series of laws were also devised to deprive Iranian women of their individual and social rights. There are many agencies in charge of suppression and specifically tasked to counter improper veiling. According to official reports, in a matter of just one year, regime agents confronted 3.6 million so-called improperly veiled women on the streets and put 18,000 of them on trial[4]. In fact, they have turned Iran into a vast prison for women.

Two years ago, agents of the clerical regime splashed acid on faces of women in Isfahan. Young women like Soheila, Neda and Sara still burn and suffer from their wounds. Their pain and suffering exemplify the agony of millions of Iranian women. For this reason, we reiterate that Iranian women must be free! They must be free to choose what they believe in, what they want to wear and how they want to live. And we repeat: NO to compulsory veiling ; NO to compulsory religion[5]; and

---

3. Read the complete text of Hassan Rouhani›s remarks in the Appendices.
4. Ahmadi Moghaddam, then commander of the State Security Force: «The Vice Patrols go after uncultured people...» He asserted that the police had dealt with 3.6 million «improperly veiled women».
Radio Farda, August 21, 2014
http://www.radiofarda.com/content/f2-iran-police-arrested-people-beach-summer-program-hijab/26542941.html
5. After meeting Maryam Rajavi, a French writer wrote an article about her views on wom-

NO to compulsory government.

Restriction of women's participation in society

Today, in addition to inequality, oppression and repression, severe poverty has overwhelmed the lives of the majority of Iran's people, particularly women. In Tehran, women sell their unborn infants for only 25 Euros[6]. The number of women sleeping in cardboard boxes in the streets of the capital exceeds 5,000[7]. Beyond such pervasive destitution, however, government policies restrict women's participation in social life more and more every day. Eighty-seven percent of the nation's unemployed are women[8]. The number of unemployed educated women has reached more than four million[9]. And over the past decade, more than 100,000 women have been fired from their jobs every year[10].

en›s veiling. The article has been included in the Appendices.

6- Siavosh Shahrivar, general director for social and cultural affairs at Tehran›s Governorate: «Some women who are addicted or sex slaves and their number is small, get pregnant. Sometimes, they sell their infants. We must accept the fact that part of the sale of infants is carried out in an organized manner... Reports indicate that women sleeping in cardboard boxes and prostitutes go to some hospitals in southern or central Tehran for delivery of their babies whom they sell after birth in return for 100-200 thousand toumans.» (The state-run Mehr news agency, February 7, 2016)

7- Fatemeh Daneshvar, chair of the social committee of Tehran›s City Council: «The phenomenon of women sleeping in cardboard boxes has been growing at a faster pace such that 5000 of the total 20,000 people sleeping in cardboard boxes in Tehran are women.» (The state-run media, May 29, 2015)

8. Vahideh Negin, advisor to the Minister of Labor, Cooperation and Social Welfare: «Some 40 million of the over 10-year-old population in the country are economically inactive. Women comprise 87 per cent of this economically inactive population. A considerable part of them, i.e. 64 per cent, are housewives.(The state-run Mehr news agency, April 28, 2015)

9. 51.02 per cent of university graduates in Iran are «inactive». The unemployment rate for female graduates in the country is 65.5 per cent. From a total of 5.305.000 female graduates, only 1.282.000 have jobs and 546.000 are looking for jobs. (The state-run Mehr news agency, January 5, 2016)

10. Women›s unemployment rate was 32.6 per cent in 2013. A year later, this figure increased by 11 per cent and reached 43.4 per cent in 2014. A glance at women›s employment over the past 10 years shows that some 100.000 women have been dismissed from the job market

Women's economic participation is less than 13 percent[11], and women's political participation is meaningless. In nine rounds of parliamentary elections over the past 36 years, a total of only 50 women have been allowed into the parliament[12]; at present they make up only 3%.

Such restrictions constitute a conscious political decision and effort by the Velayat-e Faqih regime to deny women's participation. So, I tell my sisters and daughters across our homeland: You deserve to take your life and fate into your own hands in an Iran without Velayat-e Faqih. You and your pioneering sisters in Camp Liberty can and must sweep away the mullahs' religious tyranny and all the fundamentalist groups inspired by them from the region. You can restore freedom in Iran, peace in the region and security in the world.

Iranian Resistance predicates all action on women's equal participation in political leadership

After the overthrow of the mullahs' religious tyranny, we plan to abolish the death penalty and create a democracy based on freedom, equality, and separation of religion and state.

We seek to restore women's equal rights in all areas, including their equal fundamental rights and equality before the law, in the economy, and in the family, as well as their freedom of choice in clothing, and their active and equal participation in political leadership.

The women of the Iranian Resistance are fighting so that the

---

every year. (The state-run ISNA news agency, June 30, 2015)

11. Presidential deputy on women›s affairs, Shahindokht Molaverdi: «Women›s economic participation is only 12.6 per cent and their economic revenue is so low that needs to be seriously planned.» (The state-run ISNA news agency, May 7, 2015)

12. The total number of female deputies in the parliament, from the first to the 9th Majlis, has been 78. In the nine terms of Majlis, only 50 women have been able to find their way into the parliament since 28 of them were members in repeated terms. (The state-run Young Journalists Club, May 9, 2015)

people of Iran, and especially women, can be free and able to exercise their rights in determining their own destinies. Velayat-e Faqih is a hysterical monopoly of power, that confronts this right with all its might.

In contrast, we emphasize maximum participation of women, namely their equal participation in political leadership. This is not just a motto or only a plan for Iran of the future, but a practical reality in the Resistance movement. Our Resistance movement has a leader who believes deeply in pure, democratic relations and, as such, has opened the way for the advancement of the movement for equality. Our movement has struggled for over 50 years, against two dictatorships, under the direction of a leader profoundly devoted to the theistic, just cause of equality. The PMOI has predicated all its actions and relations on the principle of equality, particularly over the past three decades.A generation of PMOI women, who for years have presided over all the major branches of this movement, have made this happen. Moreover, a generation of men who believe in the cause of equality and have accepted women's equality and leadership, have entered into a new world of emancipation and responsibility. The formation of the PMOI's Central Council, comprised of 1,000 women to lead the Resistance, has been a major stride in this path. Now, they prepare to pass their responsibilities on to the new generation.

The message of the Central Council is simple: Rejecting the notion of «me first» when presented with the opportunity to lead, but accepting the notion of «me first» when given an opportunity to sacrifice and shoulder responsibility. Instead of focusing on others' shortcomings and weaknesses, we must look at their strengths and build a new, humane world.

My dear sisters,Solidarity is our greatest asset. Let us expand our chain of unity from Iranian prisons and infernos of fear in the Middle East to wherever there is oppression. Let us send a new message of emancipation to humankind. We can and we must.

Women's Power is the Greatest Challenge to Islamic Fundamentalism

Maryam Rajavi, on International Women's Day Berlin – March 7, 2015

A grand gathering was held in Berlin on March 7, 2015, on the occasion of the International Women's Day. Mrs. Maryam Rajavi was in attendance.

A number of international dignitaries and prominent women from around the world participated, including Kim Campbell and Iveta Radicova, the former prime ministers of Canada and Slovakia; Rita Süssmuth, former speaker of the German Bundestag; Linda Chavez, former White House director of public relations; Frances Townsend, US presidential advisor on internal security and terrorism (2004-2008); Ingrid Betancourt, former presidential candidate from Columbia; Sabine Leutheusser Schnarrenberger, former Justice Minister of Germany, Maria Candida Alameida, General Prosecutor of Portugal, Khuleh Dunya, representing a women's delegation from the Syrian opposition; Najima Thay Thay, representing a delegation of female MPs from Arab countries; Valentia Leskaj, Albanian lawmaker and Vice-President of Council of Europe Parliamentary Assembly; Senator Margarita Duran Vadell and Beatriz Becerra, MEP, from Spain; Nele Lijnen, from Belgium representing a large delegation of female MEPs; and Ranjana Kumari, from India.

Other personalities participating in this rally included Rudy Giuliani, former Mayor of New York; Gunter Verheugen, European Commissioner (1999-2009); Horst Teltschik, National Security Advisor to Chancellor Helmut Kohl and former Leader of Munich Security Conference; Bishop Wolfgang Huber, former President of German Protestant Council; Otto Bernhardt, President of the Konrad-Adenauer Foundation and Chair of German Committee in Solidarity with Free Iran; Ryszard Czarnecki, Vice-President of European Parliament from Poland; Alejo Vidal Quadras, President of the International Committee in Search of Justice (ISJ); Struan Stevenson, President of the European Iraqi Freedom Association (EIFA); Bernard Kouchner, Giulio Maria Terzi, and Maia Panjikidze, former foreign ministers of France, Italy and Georgia.

Text of Maryam Rajavi's remarks in this gathering follows:

On the eve of International Women's Day, we extend our warmest greetings to the women who have arisen for the ideal of equality, made the ultimate sacrifice, opened the pathway for others and heralded a new age in our world.

I am delighted that we are holding this conference, whose focus is on tolerance and equality, in Berlin. I offer my thanks to all women's rights advocates in Germany present here, especially Mrs. Rita Süssmuth, for this gathering.

In the past two centuries, our world has time and again reached new heights in large measure due to women's equality movements. I refer to the landmark movement for women's suffrage; their efforts to obtain individual rights and freedoms, including the right to education, to ownership, to divorce, to inheritance, to equal pay, to increasing women's quota in economic and political institutions; and their selfless struggle in the liberation movements fighting against dictatorship.

Regrettably, the advancement of the ideal of equality has today come face-to-face with a formidable barrier, Islamic fundamentalism. While endangering the region and world through genocide, terrorism and discrimination, this phenomenon is most hostile to women.

For this reason, today the plight of women in the Middle East is entwined with lack of security, oppression, homelessness, murder and servitude.

Far beyond the Middle East, fundamentalism is now threatening Europe and other regions across the globe. Nevertheless, I want to say that there is a way to defeat and overcome this destructive force; there is a solution: Women's power is the greatest challenge to Islamic fundamentalism.

Indeed, the solution is being offered by a resistance movement which believes in and has proven that power and leadership, and which is led by women.

The solution to fundamentalism

Confronting fundamentalism requires a comprehensive solution, including a cultural response. By invoking the name of Islam, fundamentalism uses this religion as a weapon to go on the offensive. Thus, the answer is in democratic Islam, the antithesis to fundamentalism.

I must emphasize that these two phenomena are diametrically opposed to one another. One is a dictatorial ideology and the other is the religion of freedom, which recognizes sovereignty as the most important right of the people. One defends religious discrimination; the other is an Islam which defends equal rights for the followers of other religions. One is monopolistic and dogmatic; the other is a tolerant Islam, which promotes respect for belief in other ideas and religions. One is a religion imposed through force; the other is an Islam which rejects any compulsion in religion. One practices misogyny; the other promotes gender equality.

By underscoring this reality half a century ago, the People's Mojahedin of Iran challenged Islamic fundamentalism. Speaking about these two Islams, the Resistance's Leader Massoud Rajavi said that one interpretation of Islam «is the harbinger of darkness while the other is the standard bearer of freedom, unity and emancipation. But the battle between these two, which is at the same time a battle of destiny for the Iranian people and history, is one of the most important tests of contemporary civilisation.»

Now, we must answer this question: politically speaking, what is the solution to fundamentalism?

Today, in Asia and Africa, different fundamentalist groups are engaged in destruction and terrorism under the banner of Islam. Their atrocities, having spread to Paris, Brussels and Copenhagen, have endangered civilization. How can this danger be thwarted? Where is the core of this danger which, if destroyed, would mean the end of fundamentalism?

We must find the answer in challenging the religious dictatorship ruling Iran, because this regime is the heart of the problem and its support for Bashar Assad's dictatorship in Syria and Maliki in Iraq led to the emergence of fundamentalist militias and ISIS.

As such, silence vis-à-vis the Iranian regime's meddling in Syria, Iraq and other regional countries, let alone collaborating with it under the pretext of confronting ISIS, represents a strategic mistake. It would be delusional to ask the arsonist to put out the fire. On the contrary, the correct policy is to evict the mullahs' regime from Iraq and Syria.

The Iranian regime is the founding state for most of the atrocities and evil which fundamentalist groups have perpetrated and are perpetrating using the mullahs' rule as a model.

Indeed, who made stoning to death an official practice in the last two decades of the Twentieth Century? Who enacted into law eye gouging and limb amputation as punishment? Who massacred the largest number of political prisoners since the Second World War? Who issued a fatwa to murder a foreign author? Who revived and modelled itself on a reactionary caliphate?

Indeed, it is the velayat-e faqih regime, the godfather of terrorism, the enemy of Middle East nations and the primary threat to global peace and security. As we mark International Women's Day, I must say that Khomeini and his cronies have perpetrated many heinous crimes and assaults against women, most of which remain unaccounted even now.

The reality is that the shocking and heart wrenching crimes committed by ISIS in recent months are only a small part of the catastrophe the Iranian people have had to endure for the past 36 years. It was the mullahs' regime which initiated terrorism under the banner of Islam.

Fortunately, leaders of Western powers have unequivocally distinguished between Islam and fundamentalism. Chancellor Merkel recently said that terror under the banner of Islam was an insult to God.

Indeed, the Iranian regime serves as the founder, the patron and the guide for fundamentalism in the world today. For this reason, bringing down this regime, which acts as the godfather of ISIS, is an urgent imperative, not only for the Iranian people but for the Middle East region and the world at large.

Targeting the epicenter of Islamic fundamentalism

The international community cannot defeat fundamentalism, unless and until it targets the epicenter of fundamentalism, namely the mullahs' regime in Iran.

The Western policy of appeasement is to blame for the West not only failing to seriously confront fundamentalism, but also choosing the path of conciliation with its state sponsor, the regime in Iran, and partnering with it in clamping down on the alternative to fundamentalism.

Indeed, why are Western governments confused over how to deal with ISIS and extremism under the name of Islam? Why have they failed to correctly identify the reality of fundamentalism, its threats and its profound weaknesses? Because they are immersed in appeasing the fundamentalists.

We say to them: stop appeasement and separate your ranks from the epicenter of fundamentalism, namely the regime in Iran.

Similarly, I caution you that offering concessions to this regime in the course of the nuclear talks runs counter to the best interests of the people of Iran and the region, and undermines global peace and security. It is also tantamount to sacrificing the human rights of the Iranian people.

Just three days ago, simultaneous with the nuclear talks, the mullahs hanged publicly and secretly dozens of prisoners, including six Sunni Kurdish political prisoners who had been on hunger strike. Their execution was a bid to conceal the regime's impasse and prevent popular uprisings. We hail those martyrs and stress that silence and inaction over these inhuman crimes under the pretext of nuclear negotiations only embolden the mullahs to continue such atrocities and persist in their bomb-making projects. The mullahs came to the negotiating table out of utter desperation. But the policy of appeasement has emboldened them. Such a feeble policy amounts to encouraging fundamentalism, and Western powers must put a stop to it.

There is a solution, because the Iranian people have at no time remained silent vis-à-vis the ruling religious dictatorship. Over the past three decades, they have worked to form a democratic alternative to it.

This alternative has at its core a movement that believes in genuine and democratic Islam, and embraces the separation of religion and state. It is a powerful alternative and the harbinger of women's equality in all spheres, especially in political leadership and governance. This movement owes it perseverance and advancement to its belief in the ideal of equality.

The presence of women at all levels of this movement and their steadfastness in the frontlines of battle amid the most intense pressures and slaughter has created a new level of commitment to the ideal of equality, and by extension endowed this movement with a new level of strength and perseverance.

Indeed, a movement which finds fulfilment in its own ideal and is not deterred by the balance of power endures, advances, remains invigorated and refreshed and creates new values, which provide it with the power to persevere today and to rebuilt tomorrow. These values include giving primacy to love, affection, friendship and putting one's colleagues first. Such values are the reverse image of rivalry, envy and eliminating others. It is, in a word, love in place of hatred. It includes not losing hope and not succumbing to hardships, despite the difficulties and the length of this struggle.

I must say that these values do not belong only to Iran's pioneering women and men. They are key to progress and liberation wherever there is oppression and inequality. This is a path and a mantra which urges hope and continuing struggle. It promotes steadfastness and perseverance.

International front against Islamic fundamentalism

Liberated women in Syria, Iraq, Palestine, Tunisia, Egypt, Jordan, Yemen, Libya, Algeria, Morocco, Afghanistan, India, Pakistan, Europe, America and elsewhere around the world,
I call on all of you to form and expand a powerful front against fundamentalism, terrorism and barbarism under the name of Islam. The presence of anti-fundamentalist men in this front is of course of special significance.

When the murder of our children in Pakistan is tolerated; when the abduction of our daughters in Nigeria and the murder and widespread homelessness of women and children in Syria become routine; when no one expresses outrage at the execution of Reyhaneh Jabbari and splashing acid on the faces of our sisters in Iran, it is the force and power of women which can and must rise to the occasion.

It is the voice of women, the cries of protest by and unity among women that can and must stop this catastrophe from continuing. Because of this historic responsibility, changing the status quo is our duty and commitment and we must all work together to realize it:

whether it is women's right to equality in all spheres, or the right to choose one's clothing, or abolishing compulsory veiling, or equal participation in political leadership.

Indeed, we must create a world based on justice, freedom and equality. The creation of such a world by women is certainly possible.

To all my sisters across Iran,

To the valiant women who persevere in prisons at this very moment,

To the young women whose voices are the loudest crying out in Iran today,

To the women teachers who took part in the teachers' protest movement in large numbers these past few days,

And to my sisters who are workers, civil servants and nurses, who study at universities or high schools,

I say, today all of you carry the mantle of liberating Iran. I call on freedom-seeking women and men throughout the world to strengthen this anti-fundamentalist front in order to fight against the religious fascism ruling Iran.

Indeed, a moment in history is looming.

Despite the darkness and despair, the world will be rid of the nightmare of fundamentalism and the nations of the Middle East will be saved from this evil spell. Without doubt, united we will achieve this. We can and we must!

Hail to all of you.

Misogyny Key to Iranian Regime's Survival

Speech to a gathering of women from the Middle East and North Africa
Office of the National Council of Resistance of Iran
Berlin – March 8, 2015

On the occasion of the International Women's Day, a roundtable discussion was held in Berlin on March 8, 2015, featuring a number of political dignitaries and women's rights activists from various countries, including the United States, Canada, France, Argentina, Spain, Italy, Finland, Portugal, Romania, Albania, Palestine, Algeria, Syria, Egypt, Morocco, Jordan, Tunisia, Bahrain, Iraqi Kurdistan, Tajikistan, India, Pakistan and Moldavia.

Following are the remarks made by Mrs. Maryam Rajavi at this roundtable discussion:

On International Women's Day, I congratulate you, who have joined us from different countries.

Despite the dictatorial and misogynous conduct of the mullahs' regime in Iran, and the atrocities perpetrated by fundamentalists against our sisters in the Middle East and Africa, it is imperative that we congratulate each other on International Women's Day, this year, more than any other year, because the power of women in the movement for freedom and equality in Iran and elsewhere around the world is the fiery torch for all those who say no to dictatorship, to retrogression, and to discrimination, and are determined to eradicate them.

Compulsory veil imposed by chants of «Either the veil or a hit on the head»

In the past year, Muslim and Arab women, especially in Syria and Iraq, have come face-to-face with major challenges to their lives and destiny. For all of us, it is an imperative to understand the realities about the fundamentalists' misogyny and the role women play in confronting it. This is particularly the case because the 36-year conduct of the fundamentalists in Iran is being repeated in other countries by groups that follow them.

In the conference yesterday, I tried to briefly provide an answer to the question of a solution to fundamentalism. Today, I want to discuss fundamentalism based on the Iranian experience.

The first important reality is that misogyny is one of the major attributes of the fundamentalist dictatorship ruling Iran.

On the first anniversary of March 8th following the anti-monarchic revolution, Khomeini's betrayal of the Iranian people's revolution manifested its odious face in the streets of Tehran as his thugs clamped down on women, while calling for compulsory veiling with chants of "either the veil or a hit on the head."

The same day, women in the ranks of the People's Mojahedin, while wearing scarves, stood shoulder-to-shoulder with their sisters and challenged Khomeini's club-wielders.

Since then, Iranian women have been targeted with the most savage oppression and the most despicable humiliation and discrimination.

The torture and execution of tens of thousands of women in the ranks of the Mojahedin and other opposition groups, the overwhelming majority of them Muslim, was astounding and unprecedented.

Other restrictions for Iranian women

As far as civil liberties and individual and social rights are concerned, this regime has continuously undermined the status of women by violating international conventions, especially the Convention on the Elimination of All Forms of Discrimination Against Women.

Humiliation, detention and flogging to impose compulsory veiling on women are part and parcel of the regime's laws.

Last year, the mullahs' Supreme Leader, Khamenei, said that the notion of gender equality was a mistake. "We must totally distance ourselves from the Western way of thinking on issues such as employment and gender equality," he stressed.

For the past three years, women have been prohibited from enrolling in 70 fields of study in the universities, a doubling of the restrictions compared to the period before the ban. In addition, oppressive policies and guidelines are increasingly implemented to further push women into the home. Work and employment opportunities are incessantly closed off to Iranian women. For this reason, women's share of the labor force in Iran is only 13 percent, despite the fact that, according to government figures, more than two million women are bread winners in their families and most suffer from agonizing poverty.

On the other hand, the Supreme Leader has ordered the implementation of a plan for population growth. To this end, certain laws were adopted which prohibit the hiring of single men and women, and pressure women employees to have more children. The first and most important practical impact of this plan is to marginalize women.

Women are denied most social rights and freedoms. They are even deprived of watching sports games in stadiums and of singing in public. They are being eliminated from social activities. And they are even being controlled and interrogated over the most private aspects of their lives.

Crackdown on women under the pretext of veil facilitates suppression of the general public

The second important reality is that misogyny is at the core of the suppression of society as a whole, since preserving the ruling theocracy is predicated on it.

Such misogyny does not arise from blind, religious zealotry or efforts to safeguard societal chastity, or even preserving the foundations of the family. In fact, under the mullahs' rule, Iranian society has witnessed the crumbling of humanitarian and moral values, as well as the spread of prostitution.

Misogyny under the cloak of religion has become systematic and persistent because it is a lever to maintain the monopolistic domination of the velayat-e faqih. Misogyny is the raison d'être for dozens of the regime's suppressive agencies. It justifies the permanent surveillance operations in the streets, the actions of street patrols and the conduct of such agencies as the "Office to Combat Vice," or the "Morality Police Force" and 20 other police entities.

Similarly, clamping down on women on the pretext of mal-veiling is one of the most effective means to repress society and silence any voice of dissent.

Last autumn, in Isfahan the mullahs demonstrated their barbarism and savagery by splashing acid on the faces of women.

The mullahs have no scruples in enchaining women on so-called religious grounds. In other words, they have a free rein in scrutinizing and controlling everything, everywhere, including in sports, administrative and production settings, in hiring or firing, in constantly controlling women's and youths' travel in the streets, in arbitrary raids on people's homes, in censoring books, movies, theater and music, in filtering websites and social media, in fabricating judicial cases and in attacking parties.

This explains why enforcing the hejab has gained such prominence in the regime's policies and laws. And it explains why the mullahs openly equate a "mal-veiled" woman with being counterrevolutionary. And it explains why whenever the regime suffers a political setback on the international scene, or whenever it faces social protests and uprisings, it steps up executions and intensifies the campaign against mal-veiling.

The regime's President Hassan Rouhani declared that compulsory veiling was linked to the regime's survival. "Hejab is necessary for security," he said[1].The ruling mullahs are fully aware that if they show leniency vis-à-vis compulsory veiling or modify any of their laws and policies that oppress women, the latter's power will quickly advance and mobilize society. Indeed, the need to ensure that the velayat-e faqih regime is secure is the second important reality that helps us understand the reason for the mullahs' misogynous mindset.

Women pose the most dangerous social threat to the mullahs' regime

The third important reality is that the mullahs' regime sees the yearning for freedom and equality as the most significant threat to its existence. And this is one of the most important reasons for the mullahs' vengeance towards women.

The events of the 1979 uprising against the Shah's dictatorship were similar to the Arab Spring and the recent uprisings in the Middle East against dictatorship and corruption.

1. The Iranian state-run television, September 7, 2014.

Amid all of these, women, who have historically suffered discrimination and humiliation, have had the greatest and the most fundamental demands. And they continue to have them, namely equality and emancipation.

This is particularly the case because we are living at an age when society's real progress would only be possible through gender equality. As such, women's demands and their perseverance pose the greatest threat to the Iranian regime, which explains why the religious dictatorship ruling Iran is the record holder in the execution of women political activists in the contemporary era.

A year after the resistance against the mullahs began in Iran, some three decades ago, thousands of women were imprisoned.

In subsequent years, the mullahs perpetrated every conceivable crime against women, but Iranian women did not surrender.

This is the most important and honorable outcome of Iranian women's confrontation against the velayat-e faqih regime. The suppression is ongoing, but the mullahs have failed to impose their reactionary practices on Iranian women.

Laws on compulsory veiling continue to be implemented, but Iranian women have resisted and clashes with suppressive forces are on the rise. Repression is omnipresent, but has failed to thwart Iranian women in raising their demands.

And Iranian women's most urgent demand is change in the status quo, namely the overthrow of the velayat-e faqih regime. Indeed, in their showdown with a regime which has always sought to humiliate and eliminate Iranian women, the presence of 1,000 women in the PMOI's Central Council, who are leading the fight against religious fascism, is the most obvious affirmation of women's critical role and their sense of responsibility and competence in Iranian society. The role of women in the Iranian Resistance has been decisive in the Iranian women's confrontation with the misogynous and inhuman ruling regime. This is the model for perseverance, which calls on all women to fight for freedom and equality and to take on the responsibility of liberating society as a whole.

Dear Sisters,

I also want to underscore the great responsibility which women throughout the Middle East region must assume. The current historic confrontation has created a situation where the responsibility of women has gone far beyond their own struggle for freedom and equality.

Today, the great responsibility of saving the nations of the Middle East from the evil of fundamentalism rests on the shoulders of women. In this struggle, women's principal weapon, their greatest potential and resource, is their ever-stronger solidarity and bond among themselves. Despite different religions and nationalities, despite a variety of beliefs and cultures, despite all the differences, what can create an extraordinarily effective force is women's unity and solidarity. Thus, I again call on you to form and expand a powerful front against Islamic fundamentalism, terrorism and barbarism masquerading as Islam. From the bottom of my heart I hope and am confident that although today darkness and gloom have befallen Iran and the Middle East, women's struggle will herald a bright future, which will bestow the nations of this region with freedom, democracy and equality.

Interview by the French Magazine, Women Side

Maryam Rajavi
A New Iran?

Women Side- April 12, 2017

Présidente élue du **Conseil National de la Résistance Iranienne**, Maryam Radjavi est connue pour son opposition au régime de la République islamique d'Iran et pour ses prises de position en faveur de la démocratie, de la séparation de la religion et de l'État, et de l'égalité des femmes et des hommes. La rencontrer s'imposait.

The President-elect of the National Council of Resistance of Iran, Maryam Rajavi, is known for her opposition to the regime of the Islamic Republic of Iran and for her positions in favor of democracy, separation of religion and state, and equality of women and men. It was necessary to meet her.

What is the situation of women in Iran?

In a general overview, the situation of women in Iran can be described as this: Their great energy has been compacted and confined. They resemble a compressed spring that cannot wait to be released and to jump forward. But they are blocked by a steel-hard barrier built by the mullahs' supreme leader.

Today's Iran is one of the most oppressive regimes towards women.

Since the first day, the mullahs systematically repressed women and discriminated against them with numerous constraints.

From an economic standpoint, out of a population of 80 million in Iran, 45 million are inactive. Nearly 90% of this inactive population are women. Women are victims of a deep economic crisis which began in 2008. One-eighth of the 24 million families in Iran are headed by women, single mothers who live in complete destitution.

Over the past ten years, tens of thousands of women have lost their jobs, reducing women's economic participation to 14%. Unemployed women are twice as many as men and the sale of newborns has become a means of survival for the poorest. In Tehran, there are many streets, their walls covered with ads for the sale of newborns. There are 5,000 homeless women in the capital alone, and the number of street women grows every year.

From a legal point of view, the mullahs' Civil Code is based on discrimination against women. Women cannot become a president, a leader or a judge. They are also deprived of many other jobs. Women inherit half as much as men and their testimony in court is worth half that of a man. In some cases, their testimony has no value, at all. Even the price of blood that a murderer must pay in compensation for the murder of a woman, according to the mullahs' laws, is half that of a man. Under the mullahs' Penal Code, women's rights and worth have been reduced to half those of a man. This has opened the way for violence and murder, such as honor killings. Recently, a high-ranking mullah, Makarem Shirazi, declared, «There is always a form of masochism in some women, which for some reason is intensified sometimes. In such cases of exceptional crisis, it is good for them to be punished moderately.»

The mullahs' sharia laws have spawned a patriarchal culture by supporting decadent customs such as polygamy or temporary marriages.

The clerical regime's laws clearly sanction rape of women. The state courts do not heed the victims' appeals to justice, and those who defend themselves against such violence are hanged like Reyhaneh Jabbari, the young woman executed in Tehran in October 2015.

In the family, the wife must be subject to her husband, she has no right to divorce, and if she is divorced, she does not have custody rights. She must also ask for her husband's permission to enjoy her own property, travel, leave home or even observe certain religious rites.

Social relations are affected by sexual apartheid. Educational environments, health centers, offices and even buses are segregated to maintain the inferior status of women and deprive them of their rights and freedoms. They are even deprived of going to see matches in sports stadiums and of singing in public.

In September 2016, Khamenei announced that the role of women was to be mothers and to look after the house, and that the role of men was to be fathers and to have economic activities. He also called for the strengthening of the official policy on increasing the fertility rate.

The mullahs' principal means of repressing and humiliating women is the compulsory veil. To enforce this law, the mullahs have made sure that women do not feel safe, wherever they are, because there is permanent control on women and they are reprimanded, arrested, humiliated and punished. In 2016, the State Security Forces commander said that an average of 2000 «mal-veiled» women are arrested every day in Iran. There are more than 20 (sic.) bodies to enforce the compulsory veil.

Is the regime in Iran a misogynist regime?

Absolutely. However, I must explain what things are the reasons for the mullahs' misogyny and what things are not.

To achieve freedom and democracy, the Iranian nation overthrew the Shah's dictatorship in 1979. Liberation movements and democratic parties had been suppressed over the years. This provided exceptional circumstances for Khomeini to take advantage of their absence and usurp the leadership of the revolution. Khomeini was obscurantist and tyrannical. Therefore, as soon as he came to power, his main duty was to combat the democratic aspirations of society which were primarily carried by women. Women and especially young women had become politically aware and participated by the millions in the 1979 revolution. They rejected inequality and were not going to tolerate any more humiliation.

By repressing women, Khomeini's religious dictatorship enchained the whole society.

As for what is not the reason for the mullahs' misogyny is

their claim of intending to implement the laws of Islam. They portray Islam as a religion of inequality, constraint, repression and exploitation of women which has come to protect and reinforce patriarchy. It is a totally inverted image of Islam. Whereas the verses of the Quran put men and women on an equal footing and reject any constraint in religion. In the first years of its advent, Islam took major strides to grant women social and economic rights, a measure that was a great revolution in its time, i.e. 14 centuries ago. These were steps towards women's equality.

In a country ruled by a religious regime with such an outlook on women, how was it that a woman got to head the opposition movement?

The status of women under the religious tyranny in power in Iran is incompatible with the position they deserve and their level of awareness, intellectual progress and history of struggle.
Iranian women began their struggle for freedom and equality several decades before the 1907 Constitutional Revolution. They have made passionate efforts throughout history. Persian poetry and literature, as well as Iran's education and science have seen the emergence of many great women who presented a new image and identity of Iranian woman as a free human being who makes her own choices in life. The most dedicated efforts were made by those women who engaged in the struggle against dictatorships. They fought both for freedom of their people and to create a new identity for Iranian women who wanted to be free and independent, to take charge of their own fate, and play a decisive role in the

destiny of their country.

In the struggle against the mullahs' theocracy which is one of the most barbaric tyrannies in the history of Iran, women have played a leading and indispensable role in the torture chambers, before the firing squads as well as in the uprisings and the organized resistance movement.

Women's status and presence on various levels of leadership in the People's Mojahedin Organization of Iran (PMOI) and their occupation of more than half the seats of the Iranian Parliament-in-exile, the National Council of Resistance of Iran (NCRI), are products of women's sacrifice and trailblazing role. Iranian women have acquired their quality and competence in a long and difficult struggle on a tortuous and complicated path studded with obstacles.

Many years ago, on behalf of the Iranian Resistance, I announced women's active and equal participation in political leadership as one of the most important points of the Resistance's platform for the free Iran of tomorrow. In our view, women's leadership is not only a beautiful motto or dream, but an accessible reality because it is backed by a rich history of struggle of women who have acquired competence in a hard-fought battle against the Iranian regime.

What is your recommendation, if no action is taken in favor of women's freedom in Iran?

It is an accurate conclusion that one can never expect the clerical regime to take any small step towards restitution of women's freedoms and rights. Iran's ruling theocracy is characterized by misogyny and if it abandons repression of women and discrimination against them, it denies itself. This regime is incapable of reform. This has been proven in nearly 40 years of the regime's history. On three different occasions, a few mullahs emerged who claimed to be moderates. The first was Rafsanjani, next was Khatami and now Rouhani. But it was proven in practice that they had no mandate but to prolong the rule of this theocracy and they did not distance themselves from the regime's misogynist policies. Rafsanjani used to say that the brain of women is smaller than that of men. And some 70 women have been executed under the current president (Rouhani).

Are you planning to be Iran's president? If yes, to what extent?

The National Council of Resistance of Iran is a coalition of groups and personalities of different political convictions and tendencies, from multiple ethnic groups in Iran. It is the democratic alternative to the mullahs' religious tyranny. The NCRI has elected me as President for the transitional period after the overthrow of the clerical regime. It is a term-limited mandate that will end with the formation of the new Constitutional and Legislative Assembly and the adoption of the country's new Constitution. The future Iranian President will be elected by the Iranian people in a free election.

This Is Our History

Moments and Images of Iranian Women's Struggle and Suffering

Remarks by Maryam Rajavi in the photo exhibition
on
150 years of struggle by Iranian women
February 27, 2017 – Tirana, Albania

I deeply appreciate everyone involved in preparing this wonderful display, which reminds us of the glorious moments of the long and tortuous path the women of Iran have travelled over the years in confronting several dictatorships. It is the history of the heroism of the Iranian woman and of course, the history of her suffering.

Every one of these portraits conveys a long story Look at the portrait of Tahereh Tolou, who was stabbed in the heart by Khomeini's Revolutionary Guards and her body left hanging from a tree at Charzebar pass. Another example: the portrait of Neda Agha-Soltan, killed in the streets of Tehran.

All of these comprise our history, the history of our people's venerable fight for freedom.

I would also like to stress that only a small part of the heroism of Iranian women has been reported or registered in history, the fragments that the misogynous and dark-minded rulers were not able to censor or distort. And again, only a small part of the bitterness, wounds and pains of our sisters' 150-year struggle in Iran has been presented here, because there were no means --photographs, films, poems or novels-- to depict them.

Nevertheless, it is very important to commemorate Iranian women's legacy and history of struggle, which has continued incessantly over the years: their struggles and sacrifices; the women who were tied to beds and flogged, but staunchly resisted; the women who made discoveries and did enlightening work in all areas by writing poems or novels, or through education and scientific research; and the women who toiled as workers, farmers, nurses, etc.

This shows that the Iranian people and women's desire today for freedom and equality enjoys a long, rich and powerful history. It shows how our women's struggle has evolved, step by step, to define a pivotal role in the resistance for freedom. When you line up these portraits, it conveys this message: Iranian women's endurance will definitely turn the page of history.

No to compulsory veil, No to compulsory religion, No to compulsory government

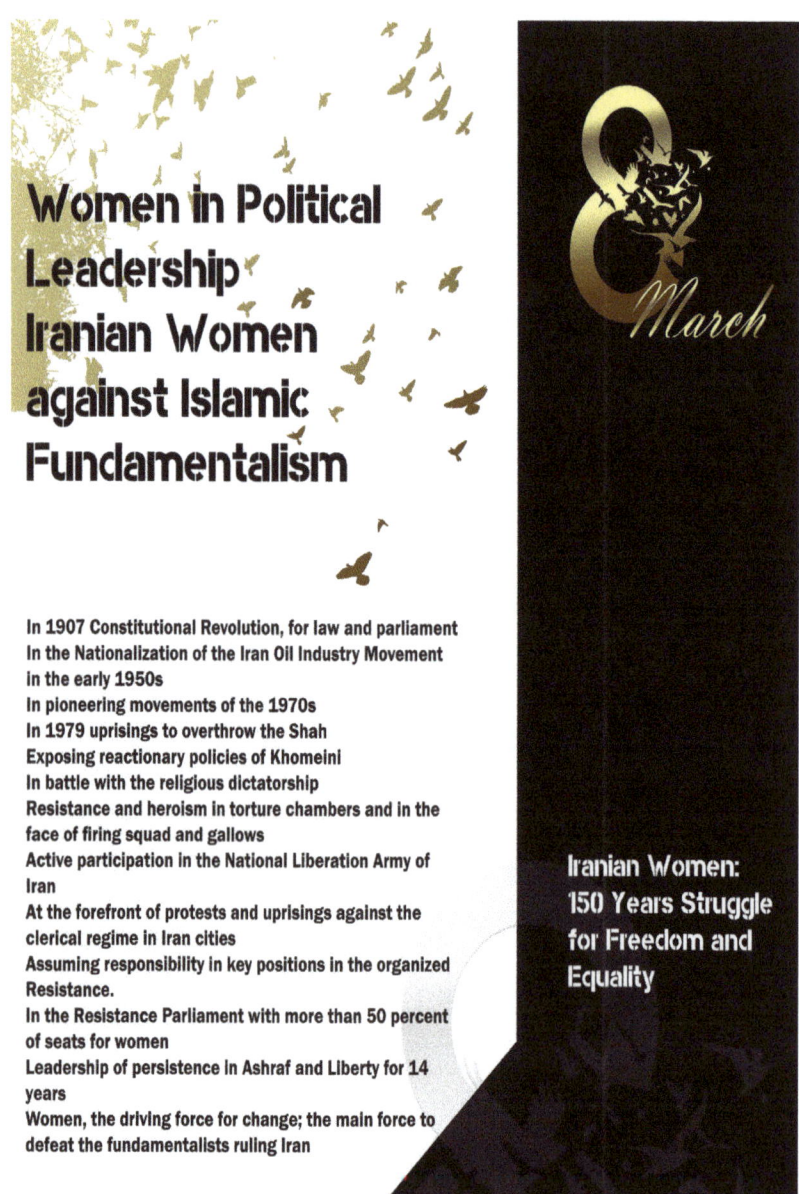

Women in Political Leadership Iranian Women against Islamic Fundamentalism

In 1907 Constitutional Revolution, for law and parliament
In the Nationalization of the Iran Oil Industry Movement in the early 1950s
In pioneering movements of the 1970s
In 1979 uprisings to overthrow the Shah
Exposing reactionary policies of Khomeini
In battle with the religious dictatorship
Resistance and heroism in torture chambers and in the face of firing squad and gallows
Active participation in the National Liberation Army of Iran
At the forefront of protests and uprisings against the clerical regime in Iran cities
Assuming responsibility in key positions in the organized Resistance.
In the Resistance Parliament with more than 50 percent of seats for women
Leadership of persistence in Ashraf and Liberty for 14 years
Women, the driving force for change; the main force to defeat the fundamentalists ruling Iran

8 March

Iranian Women: 150 Years Struggle for Freedom and Equality

Women in the Constitutional Revolution: Zeinab Pasha, heroine of the Tobacco Movement in Tabriz

Examples of publications made by women during the Constitutional Revolution and formation of women's associations during the Qajar Dynasty, after the Constitutional Revolution and later under Dr. Mohammad Mossadeq

Women's struggle, strikes, and marches against the Shah's dictatorship
1978: Massacre of people in Tehran's Jaleh Square
Freedom of the most prominent political prisoners after the people of Iran broke open the prisons: Ashraf Rajavi and Massoumeh Shademani

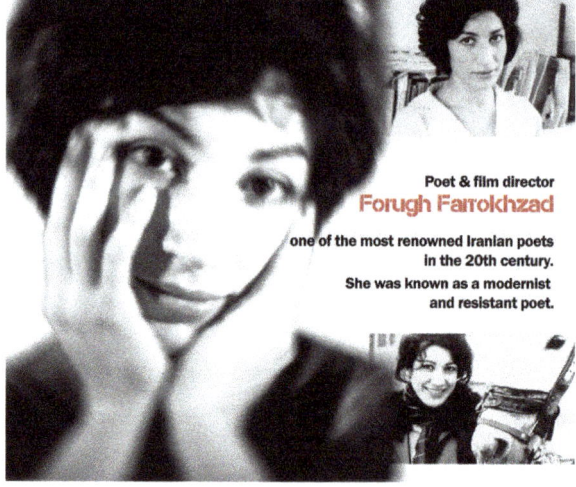

Parvin Etesami and Forough Farrokhzad, two great contemporary Iranian poets

A number of the pioneering Fedaii women who were executed by the Shah's regime

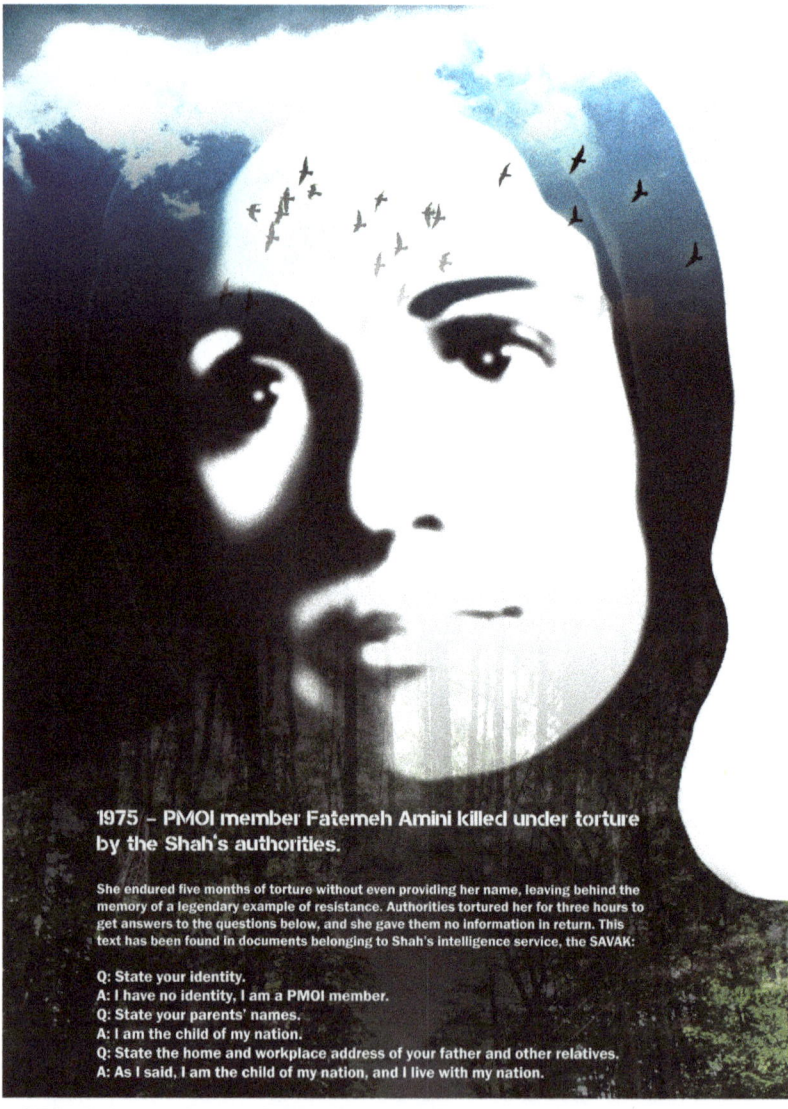

1975 – PMOI member Fatemeh Amini killed under torture by the Shah's authorities.

She endured five months of torture without even providing her name, leaving behind the memory of a legendary example of resistance. Authorities tortured her for three hours to get answers to the questions below, and she gave them no information in return. This text has been found in documents belonging to Shah's intelligence service, the SAVAK:

Q: State your identity.
A: I have no identity, I am a PMOI member.
Q: State your parents' names.
A: I am the child of my nation.
Q: State the home and workplace address of your father and other relatives.
A: As I said, I am the child of my nation, and I live with my nation.

1975: Martyrdom of PMOI member, Fatemeh Amini, under torture by the Shah's SAVAK. After five months of torture, she did not even give her name. Her mythical endurance under torture has become a legend.

23 November 1979 (Establishment of MEK Youth Groups)

Women show enormous support for MEK members following 1979 anti-monarchial revolution

Women widely embrace the PMOI after the anti-monarchic Revolution in 1979.

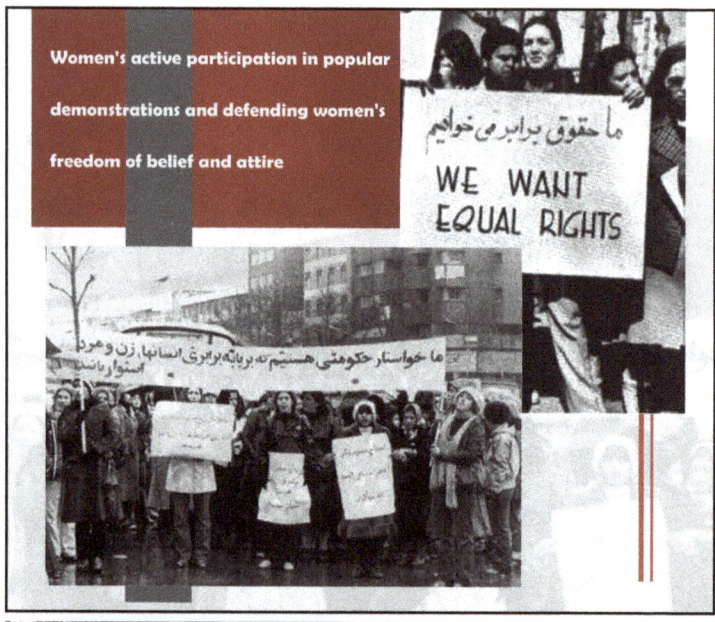

Women staged an extensive protest demonstration against suppression of freedoms and enforcement of compulsory veil by the Khomeini regime in the early days after the anti-monarchic revolution in 1979

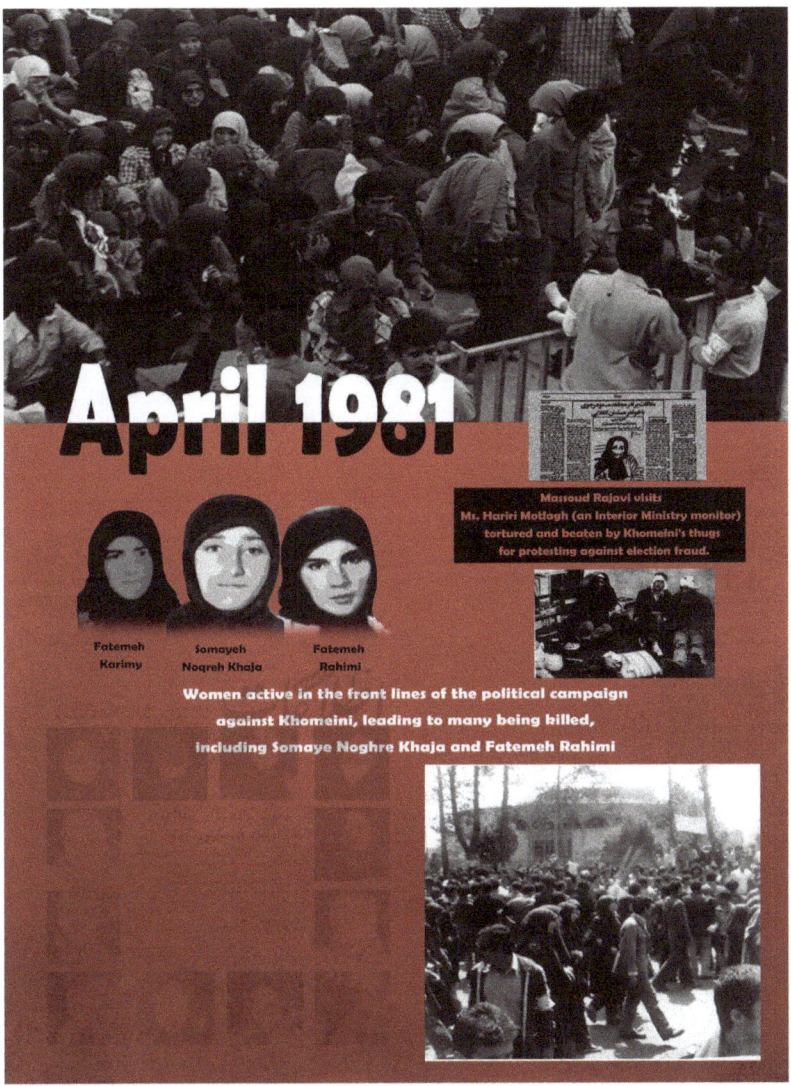

April 1981

Massoud Rajavi visits Ms. Hariri Motlagh (an Interior Ministry monitor) tortured and beaten by Khomeini's thugs for protesting against election fraud.

Fatemeh Karimy Somayeh Noqreh Khaja Fatemeh Rahimi

Women active in the front lines of the political campaign against Khomeini, leading to many being killed, including Somaye Noghre Khaja and Fatemeh Rahimi

Women were at the forefront of the political campaign against Khomeini: Somayeh Noghre-Khaja and Fatemeh Rahimi were killed in March 1981 by the regime's club wielding thugs.

Peaceful demonstration of half-a-million residents of Tehran against Khomeini on June 20, 1981. The march met with bullets by Pasdarans.

FEBRUARY 8, 1982

MEK LEADERSHIP SACRIFICING THEIR ALL AFTER FIGHTING IN THE FRONT LINES. MOUSA KHIABANI AND ASHRAF RAJAVI, ALONGSIDE OTHER MEK MEMBERS, KILLED BY KHOMEINI'S FORCES

Ashraf Rajavi and other women who were killed with her and Moussa Khiabani on February 8, 1982, fought and gave their lives for freedom on the frontline of the battle against Khomeini's Revolutionary Guards.

The arrest, torture and execution of girls under 18.Execution of Fatemeh Mesbah, 13, and torture and execution of Maryam Qodsi-Maab, 16

Memorable photos of women slain during the Eternal Light Operation

Women were at the forefront of the political campaign against Khomeini: Female candidates were nominated for parliamentary elections; women widely participated in political activities and demonstrations in protest to club wielding and repression

The clerical regime arrested, tortured and executed a large number of women, members of the PMOI and other organizations, after June 20, 1981
Execution of elderly mothers and pregnant women.

FEMALE
WARRIORS
IN COMBAT
EXERCISES
IN LIBERATION
ARMY

Shekar Mohamedzade
Medical staff and first grade nurse. Martyr of the 1988 massacre.

Forouzan Abdi Pour Pirbazari
was a university student and a member of Iran'z National Vollyball Team. After seven years of imprisonment, she was hanged during the 1988 massacre political prisoners across Iran.

27 March 1989
Monireh Rajavi,
symbol of the massacred political prisoners in 1988

Her crime: being the sister of Massoud Rajavi

From left: Monireh Rajavi, (sister of Massoud Rajavi) Forouzan Abdipour, champion of Iranian women's national volleyball team, and Shekar Mohammadzadeh, nurse; They were executed during the 1988 massacre

Crime against humanity: the 1988 massacre of 30,000 political prisoners including hundreds of women from the PMOI and other opposition groups

MEK hero Zahra Rajabi,

murdered by the mullahs' terrorists in Turkey. Rajabi is known as the martyr of defending refugees' rights

Zahra Rajabi, great martyred for refugee rights, was assassinated in Turkey by terrorists dispatched by the clerical regime from Tehran.

Presence of Madam Marzieh in military maneuvers of liberation army conducting her concert on top liberation army's tanks -1994

October 1994 - Marzieh, Diva of Persian music, sang on the tanks of the Army of Freedom

Outburst of women's fury against the clerical regime during the 2009 uprisings in Iran

Perseverance of women, PMOI members during attack on
Ashraf – 29-30 July 2009

Eight PMOI women were killed in the attack on Ashraf, April 8, 2011

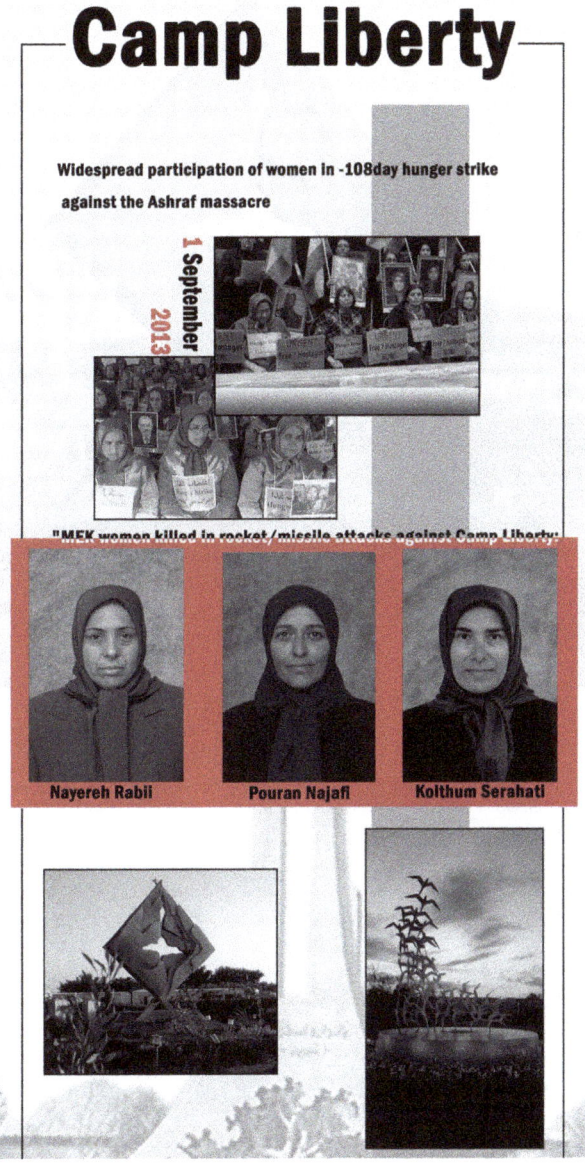

Camp Liberty

Widespread participation of women in -108day hunger strike against the Ashraf massacre

1 September 2013

"MEK women killed in rocket/missile attacks against Camp Liberty:

Nayereh Rabii

Pouran Najafi

Koithum Serahati

Three women got killed in the rocket attacks on Camp Liberty

Six PMOI women were killed in the massacre of 52 PMOI freedom fighters on September 1, 2013, on Ashraf, by mercenary agents of the Iranian regime in Iraq .

Appendices

Never give up your dreams, never!

Message of solidarity by French anthropologist, Françoise Héritier
«Pledge for Parity: Women United against Islamic Fundamentalism»
Conference in Paris – February 27, 2016

My message is very simple. It is very true that women enjoy an equal status with and similar respect as men. But this could not be achieved without struggling for it. Achieving this goal is not feasible without fighting for it and without paying its price. This is why education and training are extremely important.

At the same time, achieving political leadership is very important wherever it is possible. This is why I am very fond of the undertakings by Mrs. Maryam Rajavi. Because I quickly became aware of the quality of her struggle and her honest commitment to the separation of religion and state and to the cause of women. In some places, she has taken the initiative.

I think this is a fundamental issue, albeit related to a special environment, which can set a model for others in that she (Maryam Rajavi) chose to grant women the responsibility of exercising political leadership. This is while these types of work had traditionally been in the hands of men and women were simply just assistants or secretaries.

She decided to change the status quo. I would not say that this would be possible everywhere, for example in every company or in all countries. However, this is a model and if it turns out to be viable, and methodically it should be, there would remain no reason to claim that women are incompetent. If this experience proves to be successful, it would set a model for humanity. This will be a message to women.

An unnatural reaction has been imposed on every woman since childhood for her to say that she is never going to be able to do things because everything she does is under the dominance of men and that they should be left to men to do. Now, this new message tells women not to surrender to such impositions but that they must accept to audaciously undertake an adventure. I recommend such audacity to women of our time.

With regards to the women of (Camp) Liberty, it is very difficult for me to speak in their stead or send them a message because when I sit comfortably in my apartment in Paris, far away from wars and battles and from problems of everyday life, it would be arrogant for anyone to tell them anything. In fact, one must listen to them and follow their model. Perhaps, I could add one thing that I do very much believe in and am proud of, and it is this: not only do they need to be audacious but they should always be proud of what they are. They must powerfully present and express what they are, including to their torturers.

To today's young women, to young women and girls, -- of course I do not mean that the time is over for others, they can still continue to struggle—but to the young women who are filled with hope and seek not a dream life but a life that they dream of – these two are not exactly the same – I tell them to never abandon their dreams. Never!

The Confines of Ashraf

Message by the late Danielle Mitterrand
Read in a conference at the UN Headquarters on «The Protection of Ashraf and UN Obligations» September 21, 2011

Before giving the floor to other speakers, I would like to read a message by Mrs. Danielle Mitterrand which she wrote a few days ago in hospital. Her message is entitled, «The confines of Ashraf»:

During the Nazis' invasion of France, we were thousands of young people who had been suppressed, imprisoned, and silenced.

We dreamed of building a future where everyone could achieve their righteous place in a Europe without borders while adhering to their own culture and language and loving their own homeland.

In those days, we were called terrorists. These were also the days when I learned that the tightest, hardest and darkest confines were not the concrete, stony, or iron walls of prisons, but the confines that a dictatorship compels us to bear within ourselves: the confines of humiliation, submission and exhaustion. These barriers were forced on us to the extent that we had to deny everything and even our own identities.

Similarly, they have invented various new forms of invisible and false confines. The first is the confine of oblivion, then the confine of lies, then silence. Then, there are confines that ban your food and medicine. And, ultimately, the sonic confine, the eavesdropping poles and the electronic jamming.

Technological advances have always incited the imagination of executioners. Killing and torture, abandoning the wounded, and kidnapping innocent and defenseless hostages. This is why they think they can terminate the resistance of a nation.

In Ashraf, however, hope returns immediately because despite walls and confines, each and every one of the residents knows that thousands of their refugee sisters and brothers around the world share their hope.

And you, dear Maryam Rajavi, you represent that hope, here. So, energy returns along with love of life and the dream of a just world where everyone is guaranteed peace and security. And is the purpose of today's gathering any different from this?

At Camp Liberty, the issue is not to survive for yourself, but to live for others. This is similar to a mother's everyday sacrifice. All of us are familiar with this beautiful model as depicted by the little Shaqayeq in her letter to Ms. Pillay.

And this is the difference between the executioner and his victim, the warden and his prisoner: The latter prepares for the future while the former tries to destroy today.

My dear and lovely friends from Ashraf, tomorrow can be achieved at the price of your sacrifice. But this is not enough: Everyone must always remember the message of hope to humanity written in your blood and the example you have set for the oppressed.

Fearing the Veil

By Olivier Steiner- a French writer
November 3, 2015

Like it or not, we are terrified. Whether we are educated or ignorant, we are more or less terrified because the same story is always repeated. Fearing the ones who are not like ourselves; the Arabs, Arab kids, shanty-town dwellers, thugs, Daesh, September 11, January 11, Mali, the Hezbollah, Syria, nuclear weapons, Shariaa, the great Caliphate, ideological leaders, etc. We mix all of them with Rashida and Farida who are our next-door neighbors or live in the apartment below.

Am I exaggerating? Yes, I am, to some extent. All these things depend on where we place ourselves. It depends on where, in which city and neighborhood and with whom we live?

So, we fear the veil. We are extremely terrified (by the veil). This is unusual and contradicts our traditions. And secularism. Is there not any threats to our dear secularism amidst all this? Yes, Mrs. Maryam Rajavi, the leader of the Iranian Resistance, wears the scarf... We are taken aback... In addition, she does not shake hands with men. Again, we are shocked... What must be said? Exactly, many things... because there are two types of veil. They do not differ in color or form. But one is compulsory and forced on women; failure to observe it is ensued by the worst punishments. The other is a veil chosen freely and observed by personal choice and conviction.

Maryam Rajavi wears the scarf but she struggles for freedom of Iranian women who do not want the veil. Veiled women staged demonstrations in Iran, demanding removal of the obligation to wear the veil and they were imprisoned for this reason.

The problem is not the veil but the type of the veil. Tell me which type is your veil?

Mrs. Maryam Rajavi, a Muslim, fights for separation of religion and state and what we call secularism. She fights for equality of women and men, abolishment of the death penalty and the Shariaa laws… This, is the veil that she wears. I am not afraid of this veil. It is strange for me but this stranger is something else, a different culture and richness.

My mother and sister do not wear the veil. They are born in France and have grown up with the Christian and Jewish culture. Mrs. Rajavi is born in Tehran and she is a Muslim. My mother and sister celebrate Christmas on December 25th which is not any more dangerous than the scarves of Maryam Rajavi and her friends. It is the same. For me it is the same and it must be.

Let us fear less. Let us not mistake one veil for the other. I'd love to live in a world filled with colorful veils and miniskirts. A world where women choose whatever they want to wear.

In conclusion, I must say that France's secularism is beautiful but we must not impose it by force on other countries.

Banning the entrance of unveiled women

Rouhani: I banned the entrance of unveiled women
Excerpts from the memoirs of Hassan Rouhani,
the Iranian regime's president[1]

The issue of women's veiling and covering was not an easy one in March 1979 and preoccupied the officials for quite some time.

Government organizations and departments resumed their work after (the) February 11, 1979 (Revolution). Schools also began their activities in early March. A large number of women employees and girl students went to government offices and organizations without wearing the veil and their hair was not covered. The women who wore the veil sometimes comprised the minority among them. Some female nurses in hospitals, doctors and teachers also went to work without wearing the veil. They went to the streets with their hair not covered. Of course, there were a lot of women who wore the veil and they could be seen everywhere.

Anyway, the first time the scholars of Qom protested to women's being unveiled, they said, «Under the Islamic regime, all women must wear the veil.»

Imam (Khomeini) also referred to the need for women to wear the veil in one of his statements which led to the demonstration of unveiled women in the streets and sit-ins in front of the

---

١ - From the book «Memories of Dr. Hassan Rohani» first tome, page 571, published by Iranian revolution central publications - 1999

Justice Ministry Palace and the Prime Ministry.

At this time, Mr. Taleghani intervened and made remarks about the veil. He said, «There is no such thing as the mandatory veil. Wearing the veil is a woman's own choice.» Mr. Taleghani's views were different from the views of other scholars.

I remember the day when (the regime's incumbent president) Mr. Banisadr was visiting the Radio-Television Organization in Jam-e Jam. Unveiled women surrounded and asked him about the necessity of the veil. Elaborating on the issue, Banisadr said that women had to wear the scarf because their hair had some kind of radiation which caused this and that. These remarks surprised everyone.

Political groups and the Mujahedin-e Khalq also issued statements declaring that the veil must not be forced on women. To sum it up, as I pointed out, Mr. Taleghani said in his remarks, «We cannot force female believers into accepting the veil, but we can encourage Muslim women to wear the veil. In any case, no one can be forced to wear the veil.»

Nevertheless, we decided with friends in the Army Staff, to make the veil compulsory and begin the initiative in government ministries and offices.

The responsibility of implementing the plan to enforce the compulsory veil in the offices of the Army, was given to me. For this reason and in the first step I gathered all the women employees of the Joint Staff of the Army who were around 30. I talked to them and reached the agreement that they cover their hair by scarf while at work, beginning on the next day. Except for two or three people, all the female employees did not wear the veil, so they began nagging and creating havoc. But I stood firm and said, «From tomorrow, the guard at the entrance is obliged to prevent entry of women who do not wear the veil into the headquarters of the Army's Joint Staff.»

After the Joint Staff, it was the turn for the three forces of the Army. First, I went to the Doshan Tappeh Garrison which had a large number of women employees. Again, I called all the women to the gathering hall and spoke about the veil. Many women protested, but I decisively said, «This is an order and no disobedience is allowed.» Then I explained that we did not mean that they should wear the chador (head-to-toe black veil) and that there was no talk of chador but of covering their head and neck with a scarf.

Finally, I told them, too, that we have ordered the base's guards to prevent entry of any woman who did not observe the veil, beginning the next day.

In the Ground Force and the Naval Force, too, I spoke to the female employees. I recited some verses (from the Quran) and narrations (from the Prophet) and then spoke on the veil. I explained the issue and then showed them a directive, saying that it was an obligation for them to wear the veil.

Thank God, these efforts proved to be positive. After Nowruz holidays, all the female employees of the Army started going to work while wearing the scarf. In the ministries and government organizations and even the radio and television, the (obligation to wear the) veil was gradually implemented and all women left home while wearing the scarf.

Of course, on the days of the referendum (on the country's system of government), some women still appeared in public without the veil and went to the polling stations with their hair not covered. This social problem, however, was rapidly contained and settled in a proper manner.